# MASTERING AIR FRYER MAGIC

*Master the Art of Crispy, Crunchy, and Irresistible Air Fryer Meals*

**FANI VANOVER**

Mastering Air Fryer Magic

All rights reserved, No part of this publication may be reproduced, distributed, or transmitted in any form or by any means, including photocopying, recording, or other electronic or mechanical methods, without the prior written permission of the publisher, except in the case of brief quotations embodied in critical reviews and certain other noncommercial uses permitted by copyright law.

Copyright © FANI VANOVER 2025

Mastering Air Fryer Magic

# TABLE OF CONTENTS

Introduction To Air Fryer
    Understanding How an Air Fryer Works
    Air Fryer Essentials: Tools and Accessories
    Preparing Foods for the Air Fryer
    Temperature and Time Guidelines
    Common Air Fryer Mistakes and How to Avoid Them
    Frequently Asked Questions

CHAPTER 1: BREAKFAST AND BRUNCH MAGIC
    Classic Crispy French Fries
    Chicken Wings
    Roasted Vegetables
    Chicken Tenders
    Salmon Fillets
    Crispy Tofu
    Apple Chips

CHAPTER 2: HEALTHY AIR FRYER MEALS
    Introduction to Healthy Air Frying
    Sweet Potato Fries
    Grilled Chicken Breast
    Roasted Brussels Sprouts
    Lemon Garlic Salmon
    Veggie Burgers
    Falafel
    Zucchini Fries

CHAPTER 3: QUICK & EASY AIR FRYER RECIPES

Mastering Air Fryer Magic

Introduction to Quick & Easy Air Fryer Cooking
Grilled Cheese Sandwich
Chicken Quesadillas
Breakfast Burrito
Veggie Tacos
Garlic Bread
Stuffed Mushrooms
Nachos
CHAPTER 4: AIR FRYER SNACKS AND APPETIZERS
Introduction to Air Fryer Snacks and Appetizers
Mozzarella Sticks
Potato Chips
Buffalo Cauliflower Bites
Pigs in a Blanket
Veggie Spring Rolls
Onion Rings
Guacamole
CHAPTER 5: AIR FRYER DESSERTS
Introduction to Air Fryer Desserts
Apple Fritters
Chocolate Lava Cakes
Air Fryer Donuts
Churros
Banana Fritters
Peach Cobbler
Chocolate Chip Cookies
CHAPTER 6: AIR FRYER MEAL PREP AND EASY WEEKNIGHT DINNERS
Introduction to Air Fryer Meal Prep and Weeknight

Mastering Air Fryer Magic

- Dinners
- Chicken Thighs
- Salmon Fillets
- Veggie Stir-Fry
- Stuffed Bell Peppers
- Chicken Fajitas
- Meatballs
- BBQ Chicken Breasts

CHAPTER 7: AIR FRYER FOR SPECIAL DIETS
- Introduction to Special Diets and Air Fryer Cooking
- Keto Chicken Wings
- Vegan Tofu Bites
- Gluten-Free French Fries
- Low-Carb Zucchini Chips
- Paleo Sweet Potato Fries
- Dairy-Free Chocolate Cake
- Low-Carb Chicken Parmesan

CHAPTER 8: AIR FRYER SIDES AND SNACKS
- Introduction to Air Fryer Sides and Snacks
- Garlic Parmesan Potato Wedges
- Crispy Brussels Sprouts
- Onion Rings
- Sweet Potato Fries
- Zucchini Fries
- Baked Potatoes
- Popcorn

CHAPTER 9: AIR FRYER DESSERTS
- Introduction to Air Fryer Desserts
- Chocolate Lava Cakes

# Mastering Air Fryer Magic

Apple Fritters
Banana Bread
CONCLUSION
Mastering the Magic of Air Frying
Tips for Continuing Your Air Fryer Journey
Thank You for Choosing Air Fryer Magic!

# Introduction To Air Fryer

## Understanding How an Air Fryer Works

**The Concept:** An air fryer uses rapid hot air circulation to mimic the effect of deep frying, creating crispy textures with significantly less oil.

**Key Components:**

- Heating Element: Generates heat.
- Fan: Circulates hot air for even cooking.
- Basket/Tray: Holds food and allows air circulation.

**Why It's a Game-Changer:**

- Healthier cooking with 70–90% less oil.
- Faster cooking compared to traditional ovens.
- Versatility for frying, roasting, baking, and reheating.

## Air Fryer Essentials: Tools and Accessories

**Must-Have Tools:**

- **Tongs**: For flipping food without damaging the coating.
- **Silicone Liners**: To prevent food from sticking and simplify cleanup.
- **Oil Sprayer**: Distributes a thin, even layer of oil.
- **Meat Thermometer**: Ensures proper internal temperatures for meats.
- **Baking Dishes**: Mini pans for casseroles, cakes, or lasagna.
- **Racks**: For cooking multiple layers of food simultaneously.

### Tips for Choosing Accessories:

- Ensure accessories are heat-resistant and fit your air fryer model.
- Avoid using aluminum foil unless it's secured to prevent it from blowing into the heating element.

## Preparing Foods for the Air Fryer

### The Secret to Crispy Perfection:

- **Preheating**: Always preheat your air fryer for 3–5 minutes to ensure even cooking.
- **Oil Application**:
    - Lightly coat food with oil (use a sprayer for best results).

- Avoid over-oiling; too much oil can cause sogginess.
- **Coating and Seasoning**:
  - For crispy foods, use flour, egg, and breadcrumbs as a three-step coating process.
  - Toss vegetables with oil and seasoning before air frying.
- **Food Placement**:
  - Arrange food in a single layer for even air circulation.
  - Don't overcrowd the basket; cook in batches if needed.

## Temperature and Time Guidelines

### General Cooking Times (for reference):

- **French Fries**: 380°F (193°C) for 15–20 minutes.
- **Chicken Wings**: 400°F (204°C) for 20–25 minutes.
- **Salmon Fillet**: 370°F (188°C) for 10–12 minutes.
- **Vegetables**: 375°F (190°C) for 8–12 minutes.

### Tips for Adjusting Recipes:

- Reduce oven temperatures by 25°F when adapting recipes for the air fryer.

Mastering Air Fryer Magic

- Check food halfway through cooking to shake or flip for even browning.

## Common Air Fryer Mistakes and How to Avoid Them

Overcrowding the Basket:

- Mistake: Food doesn't crisp because there's no space for air to circulate.
- Solution: Cook in smaller batches.

Skipping Preheating:

- Mistake: Uneven cooking or longer cook times.
- Solution: Always preheat for 3–5 minutes before adding food.

Using Too Much Oil:

- Mistake: Food becomes greasy instead of crispy.
- Solution: Use a sprayer to lightly coat food.

Not Drying Foods Properly:

- Mistake: Wet foods steam instead of crisp.
- Solution: Pat foods dry before coating or seasoning.

Neglecting Cleaning:

- Mistake: Burnt oil or crumbs can create smoke and odd flavors.
- Solution: Clean the basket and tray after every use.

## Frequently Asked Questions

Do I need to use oil in an air fryer?

- Yes, for optimal crispiness, a small amount of oil is recommended.

Can I use wet batters?

- Wet batters don't work well in an air fryer. Opt for dry breading or coat lightly with a thicker batter that adheres well.

How often should I clean my air fryer?

- Clean it after every use to prevent buildup and maintain performance.

# CHAPTER 1: BREAKFAST AND BRUNCH MAGIC

## Classic Crispy French Fries

**Ingredients:**

- 4 large potatoes, peeled and cut into thin strips
- 1 tablespoon of olive oil
- Salt and pepper to taste
- Optional: garlic powder, paprika, or herbs for extra flavor

**Instructions:**

- Preheat your air fryer to 380°F (193°C).
- Place the potato strips in a bowl, drizzle with olive oil, and season with salt, pepper, and any optional spices you like.
- Toss well to coat evenly.
- Arrange the potato strips in a single layer in the air fryer basket.
- Cook for 15–20 minutes, shaking the basket halfway through for even crisping.
- Once golden and crispy, remove the fries and serve immediately.

Mastering Air Fryer Magic

**Nutritional Information (per serving):**

- Calories: 150
- Fat: 5g
- Carbs: 27g
- Protein: 3g

**Cooking Tip**: For extra crispiness, soak the potato strips in water for 30 minutes before cooking. This removes excess starch, resulting in crispier fries.

## Chicken Wings

**Ingredients:**

- 10–12 chicken wings, tips removed
- 1 tablespoon of olive oil
- 1 teaspoon of garlic powder
- 1 teaspoon of paprika
- Salt and pepper to taste

**Instructions:**

- Preheat your air fryer to 400°F (204°C).
- Pat the chicken wings dry with paper towels to ensure crispiness.
- In a bowl, toss the wings with olive oil, garlic powder, paprika, salt, and pepper until evenly coated.
- Arrange the wings in a single layer in the air fryer basket. Cook for 20–25 minutes, flipping halfway through.
- Once crispy and golden, remove and serve with your favorite dipping sauce.

**Nutritional Information (per serving):**

- Calories: 250
- Fat: 18g
- Carbs: 1g

- Protein: 22g

**Cooking Tip**: For extra crispy wings, increase the cooking time by a few minutes or use a rack inside the air fryer to allow more air circulation around the wings.

## Roasted Vegetables

**Ingredients**:

- 2 cups of mixed vegetables, chopped
- 1 tablespoon of olive oil
- 1 teaspoon of dried Italian herbs
- Salt and pepper to taste

**Instructions**:

- Preheat your air fryer to 375°F (190°C).
- Toss the vegetables in olive oil, herbs, salt, and pepper until evenly coated.
- Arrange the vegetables in the air fryer basket, ensuring they're in a single layer.
- Cook for 12 to 15 minutes, shaking the basket halfway through for even roasting.
- Once tender and slightly crispy, remove and serve.

**Nutritional Information (per serving)**:

- Calories: 120
- Fat: 7g
- Carbs: 15g
- Protein: 2g

Mastering Air Fryer Magic

**Cooking Tip**: For more flavor, add a sprinkle of Parmesan cheese over the vegetables halfway through cooking.

## Chicken Tenders

**Ingredients**:

- 2 chicken breasts, sliced into strips
- ½ cup of breadcrumbs
- ¼ cup of grated Parmesan cheese
- 1 egg, beaten
- Salt and pepper to taste

**Instructions**:

- Preheat your air fryer to 375°F (190°C).
- In a shallow dish, combine breadcrumbs, Parmesan cheese, salt, and pepper.
- Dip each chicken strip into the beaten egg, then coat with the breadcrumb mixture.
- Arrange the breaded chicken strips in the air fryer basket. Cook for 10 to 12 minutes, flipping halfway through.
- Once golden and crispy, remove and serve with your favorite dipping sauce.

**Nutritional Information (per serving)**:

- Calories: 280
- Fat: 14g
- Carbs: 12g
- Protein: 28g

**Cooking Tip**: For a gluten-free version, substitute the breadcrumbs with gluten-free breadcrumbs or crushed almonds.

Mastering Air Fryer Magic

## Salmon Fillets

**Ingredients:**

- 2 salmon fillets
- 1 tablespoon of olive oil
- 1 teaspoon of lemon zest
- 1 teaspoon of garlic powder
- Salt and pepper to taste

**Instructions:**

- Preheat your air fryer to 370°F (188°C).
- Drizzle the salmon fillets with olive oil and season with lemon zest, garlic powder, salt, and pepper.
- Place the fillets in the air fryer basket, skin-side down. Cook for 10 to 12 minutes or until the salmon is cooked through and flakes easily with a fork.
- Remove and serve with a squeeze of fresh lemon juice.

**Nutritional Information (per serving):**

- Calories: 250
- Fat: 14g
- Carbs: 1g
- Protein: 26g

**Cooking Tip**: To prevent the salmon from sticking to the basket, line it with a piece of parchment paper or lightly grease it with cooking spray.

## Crispy Tofu

**Ingredients:**

- 1 block firm tofu, pressed and cubed
- 2 tablespoons of soy sauce
- 1 tablespoon of cornstarch
- 1 teaspoon of sesame oil

**Instructions:**

- Preheat your air fryer to 375°F (190°C).
- Toss the tofu cubes with soy sauce, cornstarch, and sesame oil until evenly coated.
- Arrange the tofu in a single layer in the air fryer basket.
- Cook for 15 to 18 minutes, shaking halfway through to ensure the tofu cooks evenly.
- Once crispy, remove and serve with dipping sauce or as a topping for salads and bowls.

**Nutritional Information (per serving):**

- Calories: 150
- Fat: 9g
- Carbs: 10g
- Protein: 12g

Mastering Air Fryer Magic

**Cooking Tip**: For an extra crispy texture, press the tofu for at least 30 minutes before cooking to remove excess moisture.

## Apple Chips

**Ingredients:**

- 2 apples, thinly sliced
- 1 teaspoon of cinnamon
- ½ teaspoon of sugar (optional)

**Instructions:**

- Preheat your air fryer to 350°F (175°C).
- Arrange the apple slices in a single layer in the air fryer basket.
- Sprinkle the cinnamon and sugar (if using) over the apple slices.
- Cook for 10 minutes, flipping halfway through.
- Once crisp and golden, remove and serve as a snack.

**Nutritional Information (per serving):**

- Calories: 80
- Fat: 0g
- Carbs: 22g
- Protein: 1g

Mastering Air Fryer Magic

**Cooking Tip**: For best results, use firm, tart apples like Granny Smith, as they hold their shape better during cooking.

This chapter gives you a solid foundation of easy-to-follow recipes to start your air fryer journey. Each recipe is the secret to air fryer magic cooking and it helps you get the most out of your air fryer, whether you're cooking snacks, side dishes, or main meals.

# CHAPTER 2: HEALTHY AIR FRYER MEALS

## Introduction to Healthy Air Frying

Air frying offers a healthier alternative to traditional frying methods by using little to no oil, allowing you to enjoy the crispy textures you love without the added fat. The rapid hot air circulation not only cooks food faster but also retains more nutrients compared to other cooking methods like deep frying or boiling. Whether you're looking to make low-calorie meals, lower your cholesterol, or simply eat more vegetables, the air fryer can make it easy to prepare health-conscious dishes that are just as delicious.

## Sweet Potato Fries

**Ingredients**:

- 2 large sweet potatoes, peeled and cut into fries
- 1 tablespoon of olive oil
- ½ teaspoon of paprika
- ½ teaspoon of garlic powder

- Salt and pepper to taste

**Instructions:**

- Preheat your air fryer to 375°F (190°C).
- Toss the sweet potato fries with olive oil, paprika, garlic powder, salt, and pepper until well coated.
- Arrange the fries in a single layer in the air fryer basket.
- Cook for 15 to 20 minutes, shaking the basket halfway through for even crisping.
- Remove and serve immediately.

**Nutritional Information (per serving):**

- Calories: 160
- Fat: 6g
- Carbs: 25g
- Protein: 2g

**Cooking Tip:** Sweet potatoes cook more evenly when cut into uniform pieces, so take the time to slice them consistently.

## Grilled Chicken Breast

**Ingredients:**

- 2 boneless, skinless chicken breasts
- 1 tablespoon of olive oil
- 1 teaspoon of dried oregano
- 1 teaspoon of garlic powder
- Salt and pepper to taste

**Instructions:**

- Preheat the air fryer to 375°F (190°C).
- Rub the chicken breasts with olive oil, oregano, garlic powder, salt, and pepper.
- Place the chicken breasts in the air fryer basket, cooking for 12 minutes, flipping halfway through.
- Check that the internal temperature has reached 165°F (74°C) before removing. Serve immediately.

**Nutritional Information (per serving):**

- Calories: 240
- Fat: 10g
- Carbs: 1g
- Protein: 36g

Mastering Air Fryer Magic

**Cooking Tip**: To keep the chicken juicy, avoid overcooking. Using a meat thermometer ensures it's perfectly done.

## Roasted Brussels Sprouts

**Ingredients:**

- 2 cups Brussels sprouts, trimmed and halved
- 1 tablespoon of olive oil
- ½ teaspoon of garlic powder
- Salt and pepper to taste

**Instructions:**

- Preheat the air fryer to 375°F (190°C).
- Toss the Brussels sprouts with olive oil, garlic powder, salt, and pepper until evenly coated.
- Arrange in a single layer in the air fryer basket and cook for 12 to 15 minutes, shaking halfway through.
- Remove and serve.

**Nutritional Information (per serving):**

- Calories: 130
- Fat: 9g
- Carbs: 12g
- Protein: 4g

Mastering Air Fryer Magic

**Cooking Tip**: For extra crispiness, increase the cooking time by 3–5 minutes or add a drizzle of balsamic vinegar before serving.

## Lemon Garlic Salmon

**Ingredients:**

- 2 salmon fillets
- 1 tablespoon of olive oil
- 1 teaspoon of lemon zest
- 1 teaspoon of garlic powder
- Salt and pepper to taste

**Instructions:**

- Preheat the air fryer to 370°F (188°C).
- Rub the salmon fillets with olive oil, lemon zest, garlic powder, salt, and pepper.
- Place the fillets in the air fryer, skin-side down, and cook for 10–12 minutes, or until the salmon flakes easily.
- Serve with a lemon wedge.

**Nutritional Information (per serving):**

- Calories: 220
- Fat: 14g
- Carbs: 1g
- Protein: 26g

**Cooking Tip:** For an extra burst of flavor, drizzle the fillets with fresh lemon juice before serving.

## Veggie Burgers

**Ingredients:**

- 1 can black beans, drained and mashed
- ½ cup of breadcrumbs
- ¼ cup of grated carrot
- ¼ cup of chopped onion
- 1 tablespoon of soy sauce
- ½ teaspoon of cumin
- Salt and pepper to taste

**Instructions:**

- Preheat your air fryer to 375°F (190°C).
- In a bowl, combine the mashed black beans, breadcrumbs, grated carrot, onion, soy sauce, cumin, salt, and pepper.
- Form the mixture into patties.
- Cook in the air fryer for 10–12 minutes, flipping halfway through.
- Serve on a whole-wheat bun with your favorite toppings.

**Nutritional Information (per serving):**

- Calories: 180
- Fat: 4g
- Carbs: 30g

- Protein: 8g

**Cooking Tip**: Use a silicone baking mat to prevent the burgers from sticking to the basket.

## Falafel

**Ingredients:**

- 1 can of chickpeas, drained and mashed
- ¼ cup of onion, finely chopped
- 1 tablespoon of fresh parsley, chopped
- 1 teaspoon of cumin
- ½ teaspoon of coriander
- 1 tablespoon of olive oil
- Salt and pepper to taste

**Instructions:**

- Preheat the air fryer to 375°F (190°C).
- Combine the chickpeas, onion, parsley, cumin, coriander, olive oil, salt, and pepper in a bowl.
- Form the mixture into small balls or patties.
- Cook in the air fryer for 10–12 minutes, flipping halfway through.
- Serve with a side of hummus or yogurt dip.

**Nutritional Information (per serving):**

- Calories: 150
- Fat: 6g
- Carbs: 20g
- Protein: 6g

Mastering Air Fryer Magic

**Cooking Tip**: For a crispier texture, spray the falafel with a light mist of oil before cooking.

## Zucchini Fries

**Ingredients:**

- 2 medium of zucchini, cut into fries
- ½ cup of breadcrumbs
- ¼ cup of grated Parmesan cheese
- 1 egg, beaten
- Salt and pepper to taste

**Instructions:**

- Preheat the air fryer to 375°F (190°C).
- Dip each zucchini fry into the egg, then coat with the breadcrumb and Parmesan mixture.
- Arrange the zucchini fries in a single layer in the air fryer basket.
- Cook for 10–12 minutes, flipping halfway through.
- Serve immediately with marinara sauce.

**Nutritional Information (per serving):**

- Calories: 120
- Fat: 7g
- Carbs: 15g
- Protein: 4g

**Cooking Tip**: For an extra crispy coating, double coat the zucchini fries.

# CHAPTER 3: QUICK & EASY AIR FRYER RECIPES

## Introduction to Quick & Easy Air Fryer Cooking

Air fryers are perfect for quick meals that don't require a lot of prep or cooking time. Whether you're cooking for one or preparing a family meal, these recipes are designed to be made in 30 minutes or less. These fast, flavorful recipes will help you whip up a meal in no time, allowing you to enjoy the benefits of air frying without spending hours in the kitchen.

## Grilled Cheese Sandwich

**Ingredients**:

- 2 slices of bread
- 2 tablespoons of butter
- 2 slices of cheese (cheddar, American, or your choice)

**Instructions**:

- Preheat the air fryer to 375°F (190°C).
- Butter the outside of the bread slices. Place cheese between the slices.
- Place the sandwich in the air fryer basket. Cook for 5–6 minutes, flipping halfway through.
- Once golden and crispy, remove and serve.

**Nutritional Information (per serving)**:

- Calories: 300
- Fat: 20g
- Carbs: 28g
- Protein: 12g

**Cooking Tip**: For a healthier version, use whole-grain bread and low-fat cheese.

## Chicken Quesadillas

**Ingredients:**

- 2 flour tortillas
- ½ cup of cooked chicken breast, shredded
- ½ cup of shredded cheese
- 1 tablespoon of sour cream

**Instructions:**

- Preheat the air fryer to 375°F (190°C).
- Place the chicken and cheese between the tortillas.
- Place the quesadilla in the air fryer and cook for 6 minutes, flipping halfway through.
- Serve with sour cream and salsa.

**Nutritional Information (per serving):**

- Calories: 350
- Fat: 18g
- Carbs: 32g
- Protein: 18g

**Cooking Tip**: Cut the quesadilla into wedges for easy sharing.

## Breakfast Burrito

**Ingredients:**

- 1 flour tortilla
- 2 scrambled eggs
- ¼ cup of cooked sausage or bacon
- ¼ cup of shredded cheese

**Instructions:**

- Preheat the air fryer to 375°F (190°C).
- Scramble the eggs and mix in the cooked sausage or bacon.
- Place the egg mixture in the center of the tortilla, sprinkle with cheese, and roll it up.
- Cook for 5–7 minutes until the burrito is golden and crispy.

**Nutritional Information (per serving):**

- Calories: 300
- Fat: 20g
- Carbs: 28g
- Protein: 14g

**Cooking Tip**: Add fresh veggies like bell peppers and onions for added flavor.

## Veggie Tacos

**Ingredients:**

- 2 soft corn tortillas
- ½ cup of black beans, cooked
- ¼ cup of corn kernels
- ¼ cup of diced tomatoes
- 1 tablespoon of avocado, mashed

**Instructions:**

- Preheat the air fryer to 375°F (190°C).
- Heat the black beans and corn in the air fryer for 3–5 minutes.
- Assemble the tacos with beans, corn, tomatoes, and avocado.
- Serve with your favorite taco toppings.

**Nutritional Information (per serving):**

- Calories: 220
- Fat: 7g
- Carbs: 34g
- Protein: 7g

**Cooking Tip:** Top with a squeeze of lime juice for extra flavor.

## Garlic Bread

**Ingredients:**

- 4 slices of Italian bread
- 2 tablespoons of butter, softened
- 1 teaspoon of garlic powder
- 1 tablespoon of parsley

**Instructions:**

- Preheat the air fryer to 350°F (175°C).
- Spread butter on each slice of bread and sprinkle with garlic powder and parsley.
- Cook in the air fryer for 5–6 minutes, until golden brown.

**Nutritional Information (per serving):**

- Calories: 150
- Fat: 8g
- Carbs: 20g
- Protein: 3g

**Cooking Tip**: For extra crispy edges, use a thicker cut of bread.

## Stuffed Mushrooms

**Ingredients:**

- 8 large mushrooms, stems removed
- ¼ cup of cream cheese
- ¼ cup of grated Parmesan cheese
- 1 tablespoon of garlic, minced
- 1 tablespoon of breadcrumbs

**Instructions:**

- Preheat the air fryer to 375°F (190°C).
- Stuff the mushroom caps with cream cheese, Parmesan, garlic, and breadcrumbs.
- Cook for 8–10 minutes, until the mushrooms are tender and golden.

**Nutritional Information (per serving):**

- Calories: 120
- Fat: 9g
- Carbs: 7g
- Protein: 5g

**Cooking Tip:** Use a toothpick to secure the filling in place if needed.

## Nachos

**Ingredients:**

- 1 cup of tortilla chips
- ½ cup of shredded cheese
- ¼ cup of jalapeños, sliced
- 1 tablespoon of sour cream

**Instructions:**

- Preheat the air fryer to 375°F (190°C).
- Layer the tortilla chips in the air fryer basket and top with cheese and jalapeños.
- Cook for 5 to 7 minutes, until the cheese is melted.
- Serve with sour cream.

**Nutritional Information (per serving):**

- Calories: 250
- Fat: 14g
- Carbs: 28g
- Protein: 6g

**Cooking Tip**: Add guacamole for a delicious extra topping.

# CHAPTER 4: AIR FRYER SNACKS AND APPETIZERS

## Introduction to Air Fryer Snacks and Appetizers

Air fryers are perfect for preparing snacks and appetizers that are crispy, flavorful, and easy to make. Whether you're hosting a party or simply craving a snack, these air fryer recipes will help you make bite-sized, crunchy treats with minimal effort. From chips to dips, and everything in between, the air fryer can turn everyday ingredients into mouthwatering appetizers.

## Mozzarella Sticks

**Ingredients:**

- 8 mozzarella sticks
- ¼ cup of all-purpose flour
- 1 egg, beaten
- ½ cup of breadcrumbs
- ¼ teaspoon of garlic powder
- ¼ teaspoon of Italian seasoning

Mastering Air Fryer Magic

**Instructions:**

- Preheat the air fryer to 375°F (190°C).
- Dredge the mozzarella sticks in flour, dip in the egg, and then coat in breadcrumbs mixed with garlic powder and Italian seasoning.
- Arrange the sticks in a single layer in the air fryer basket and cook for 6–8 minutes, until golden and crispy.
- Serve with marinara sauce for dipping.

**Nutritional Information (per serving):**

- Calories: 200
- Fat: 12g
- Carbs: 18g
- Protein: 12g

**Cooking Tip**: For an extra crispy exterior, freeze the mozzarella sticks for 10 minutes before cooking.

## Potato Chips

**Ingredients**:

- 2 medium potatoes, thinly sliced
- 1 tablespoon of olive oil
- Salt to taste

**Instructions**:

- Preheat the air fryer to 360°F (182°C).
- Toss the potato slices with olive oil and salt.
- Arrange the slices in a single layer in the air fryer basket, working in batches if needed.
- Cook for 10–12 minutes, shaking halfway through, until the chips are crispy and golden.
- Let them cool for a minute before serving.

**Nutritional Information (per serving)**:

- Calories: 150
- Fat: 7g
- Carbs: 22g
- Protein: 2g

**Cooking Tip**: To make even crispier chips, use a mandoline slicer to ensure uniform thickness.

## Buffalo Cauliflower Bites

**Ingredients:**

- 1 medium cauliflower, cut into florets
- ¼ cup of buffalo sauce
- ¼ cup of breadcrumbs
- ¼ teaspoon of garlic powder

**Instructions:**

- Preheat the air fryer to 375°F (190°C).
- Toss the cauliflower florets in buffalo sauce and then coat in breadcrumbs mixed with garlic powder.
- Arrange in a single layer in the air fryer basket and cook for 10–12 minutes, shaking halfway through.
- Serve with a side of blue cheese or ranch dressing.

**Nutritional Information (per serving):**

- Calories: 130
- Fat: 7g
- Carbs: 16g
- Protein: 3g

Mastering Air Fryer Magic

**Cooking Tip**: For an extra kick, add a dash of cayenne pepper to the buffalo sauce.

## Pigs in a Blanket

**Ingredients:**

- 1 package of mini sausages
- 1 sheet puff pastry or crescent roll dough
- 1 egg, beaten (for egg wash)

**Instructions:**

- Preheat the air fryer to 375°F (190°C).
- Cut the dough into small strips and wrap them around the mini sausages.
- Brush the wrapped sausages with the beaten egg for a golden finish.
- Arrange in the air fryer basket and cook for 7–9 minutes until golden and puffed.
- Serve with mustard or ketchup.

**Nutritional Information (per serving):**

- Calories: 250
- Fat: 20g
- Carbs: 15g
- Protein: 10g

**Cooking Tip**: Use crescent roll dough for a flakier, crispier result.

## Veggie Spring Rolls

**Ingredients**:

- 1 cup of shredded cabbage
- ½ cup of shredded carrots
- ¼ cup of chopped green onions
- 8 spring of roll wrappers
- 1 tablespoon of soy sauce
- 1 tablespoon of sesame oil

**Instructions**:

- Preheat the air fryer to 370°F (188°C).
- In a bowl, mix the cabbage, carrots, green onions, soy sauce, and sesame oil.
- Fill each spring roll wrapper with the veggie mixture and roll tightly.
- Arrange the rolls in the air fryer basket and cook for 8–10 minutes, turning halfway through.
- Serve with a dipping sauce of your choice.

**Nutritional Information (per serving)**:

- Calories: 120
- Fat: 5g
- Carbs: 18g
- Protein: 2g

**Cooking Tip**: Don't overfill the spring rolls to avoid tearing the wrapper during cooking.

Mastering Air Fryer Magic

## Onion Rings

**Ingredients**:

- 1 large onion, sliced into rings
- ½ cup of flour
- 1 egg, beaten
- ½ cup of breadcrumbs
- ¼ teaspoon of paprika
- Salt and pepper to taste

**Instructions**:

- Preheat the air fryer to 375°F (190°C).
- Dredge the onion rings in flour, dip in the egg, and coat with breadcrumbs mixed with paprika, salt, and pepper.
- Arrange the rings in a single layer in the air fryer basket.
- Cook for 8–10 minutes, flipping halfway through.
- Serve with ketchup or a dipping sauce.

**Nutritional Information (per serving)**:

- Calories: 180
- Fat: 7g
- Carbs: 26g
- Protein: 3g

**Cooking Tip**: Make sure the onion rings are spaced out in the basket for an even cook.

## Guacamole

**Ingredients:**

- 2 ripe avocados
- ¼ cup of red onion, finely chopped
- 1 small tomato, diced
- 1 tablespoon of lime juice
- Salt and pepper to taste

**Instructions:**

- Cut the avocados in half, remove the pit, and scoop the flesh into a bowl.
- Mash the avocado with a fork until smooth but slightly chunky.
- Add the onion, tomato, lime juice, salt, and pepper.
- Stir to combine and serve with tortilla chips.

**Nutritional Information (per serving):**

- Calories: 160
- Fat: 14g
- Carbs: 9g
- Protein: 2g

**Cooking Tip**: To prevent browning, add more lime juice or cover tightly with plastic wrap.

# CHAPTER 5: AIR FRYER DESSERTS

## Introduction to Air Fryer Desserts

The air fryer isn't just for savory meals—it can also create delicious, crispy, and indulgent desserts in a fraction of the time it takes to bake them in the oven. These sweet treats are perfect for satisfying your cravings without the added hassle. From cookies to cakes, these recipes make use of the air fryer's ability to create golden, crisp exteriors while keeping the inside soft and decadent.

## Apple Fritters

**Ingredients:**

- 2 apples, peeled and diced
- 1 cup of all-purpose flour
- ¼ cup of sugar
- ½ teaspoon sugar of cinnamon
- ½ teaspoon of baking powder
- 1 egg
- ¼ cup of milk

Mastering Air Fryer Magic

**Instructions:**

- Preheat the air fryer to 375°F (190°C).
- In a bowl, mix the flour, sugar, cinnamon, baking powder, egg, and milk.
- Fold in the diced apples.
- Drop spoonfuls of the batter into the air fryer basket, cooking for 6–8 minutes until golden and crisp.
- Serve warm with powdered sugar on top.

**Nutritional Information (per serving):**

- Calories: 180
- Fat: 8g
- Carbs: 25g
- Protein: 3g

**Cooking Tip**: Serve with vanilla ice cream for an indulgent dessert.

## Chocolate Lava Cakes

**Ingredients:**

- ½ cup of dark chocolate chips
- ¼ cup of butter
- ¼ cup of sugar
- 1 egg
- ¼ teaspoon of vanilla extract
- 2 tablespoons of flour

**Instructions:**

- Preheat the air fryer to 375°F (190°C).
- Melt the chocolate and butter together in the microwave.
- Stir in the sugar, egg, vanilla, and flour.
- Pour the batter into greased ramekins and cook for 8–10 minutes, until the edges are set but the center remains soft.
- Serve with whipped cream or ice cream.

**Nutritional Information (per serving):**

- Calories: 250
- Fat: 18g
- Carbs: 28g
- Protein: 3g

**Cooking Tip**: Allow the cakes to cool slightly before removing them from the ramekins to avoid breaking.

## Air Fryer Donuts

**Ingredients:**

- 1 can refrigerated biscuit dough
- ¼ cup of sugar
- 1 teaspoon of cinnamon
- 2 tablespoons of melted butter

**Instructions:**

- Preheat the air fryer to 350°F (175°C).
- Cut holes in the center of the biscuit dough to form donuts.
- Brush the donuts with melted butter and cook for 5–6 minutes, until golden brown.
- Mix the sugar and cinnamon together and coat the warm donuts in the mixture.

**Nutritional Information (per serving):**

- Calories: 180
- Fat: 10g
- Carbs: 22g
- Protein: 2g

**Cooking Tip**: Serve immediately for the best texture.

## Churros

**Ingredients:**

- 1 cup water
- ¼ cup of butter
- ¼ teaspoon of salt
- 1 cup of all-purpose flour
- 2 eggs
- ¼ cup of sugar
- 1 teaspoon of cinnamon

**Instructions:**

- Preheat the air fryer to 375°F (190°C).
- Bring water, butter, and salt to a boil. Add the flour and stir until the mixture thickens.
- Remove from heat and add the eggs, one at a time.
- Pipe the dough into churro shapes and cook for 6–8 minutes until golden.
- Mix the cinnamon and sugar, then coat the churros.

**Nutritional Information (per serving):**

- Calories: 200
- Fat: 12g
- Carbs: 26g

Mastering Air Fryer Magic

- Protein: 2g

**Cooking Tip**: For extra crispy churros, spray them with a light layer of oil before cooking.

## Banana Fritters

**Ingredients:**

- 2 ripe of bananas, mashed
- ½ cup of flour
- ¼ cup of sugar
- ½ teaspoon of cinnamon
- ¼ teaspoon of baking powder
- 1 egg

**Instructions:**

- Preheat the air fryer to 375°F (190°C).
- Mix the mashed bananas, flour, sugar, cinnamon, baking powder, and egg into a batter.
- Drop spoonfuls of the batter into the air fryer basket and cook for 5–7 minutes, until golden.
- Dust with powdered sugar and serve warm.

**Nutritional Information (per serving):**

- Calories: 170
- Fat: 6g
- Carbs: 28g
- Protein: 3g

**Cooking Tip**: Serve with honey or caramel sauce for added sweetness.

## Peach Cobbler

**Ingredients:**

- 1 can sliced peaches in syrup, drained
- ½ cup of flour
- ¼ cup of sugar
- 1 teaspoon of baking powder
- ¼ cup of milk
- ¼ teaspoon of cinnamon

**Instructions:**

- Preheat the air fryer to 350°F (175°C).
- Spread the peaches in a greased air fryer-safe dish.
- Mix the flour, sugar, baking powder, milk, and cinnamon, then pour over the peaches.
- Cook for 10–12 minutes until golden and bubbly.
- Serve with a scoop of vanilla ice cream.

**Nutritional Information (per serving):**

- Calories: 180
- Fat: 8g
- Carbs: 25g
- Protein: 3g

**Cooking Tip**: You can also top the cobbler with a crumble topping for extra crunch.

## Chocolate Chip Cookies

**Ingredients:**

- 1 cup of butter, softened
- ¾ cup of sugar
- 1 cup of brown sugar
- 2 eggs
- 1 teaspoon of vanilla extract
- 2 cups all-purpose flour
- 1 teaspoon of baking soda
- ½ teaspoon of salt
- 1 cup chocolate chips

**Instructions:**

- Preheat the air fryer to 350°F (175°C).
- Cream the butter and sugars, then add eggs and vanilla.
- Mix the dry ingredients and fold into the wet ingredients, followed by chocolate chips.
- Scoop the dough into balls and arrange in the air fryer basket.
- Cook for 8–10 minutes until golden brown.

**Nutritional Information (per serving):**

- Calories: 220
- Fat: 12g

- Carbs: 28g
- Protein: 3g

**Cooking Tip**: For uniform-sized cookies, use a cookie scoop.

# CHAPTER 6: AIR FRYER MEAL PREP AND EASY WEEKNIGHT DINNERS

## Introduction to Air Fryer Meal Prep and Weeknight Dinners

When life gets busy, the air fryer becomes your best friend in the kitchen. It can help you prepare meals in a fraction of the time it would take using traditional methods, making it an essential tool for weeknight dinners and meal prep. In this chapter, we'll focus on quick, flavorful meals that are perfect for busy nights when you need something delicious without the long wait.

### Chicken Thighs

**Ingredients:**

- 4 bone-in, skin-on chicken thighs
- 2 tablespoons of olive oil
- 1 teaspoon of garlic powder
- 1 teaspoon of smoked paprika
- Salt and pepper to taste

## Instructions:

- Preheat the air fryer to 380°F (193°C).
- Rub the chicken thighs with olive oil, garlic powder, paprika, salt, and pepper.
- Arrange the chicken thighs in the air fryer basket, skin side down.
- Cook for 25–30 minutes, flipping halfway through, until the skin is crispy and the internal temperature reaches 165°F (74°C).
- Let rest for a few minutes before serving.

## Nutritional Information (per serving):

- Calories: 250
- Fat: 18g
- Carbs: 0g
- Protein: 22g

**Cooking Tip**: For an extra crispy skin, air fry the chicken thighs skin-side down first and then flip them at the halfway mark.

## Salmon Fillets

**Ingredients**:

- 2 salmon of fillets
- 1 tablespoon of olive oil
- 1 teaspoon of lemon zest
- 1 teaspoon of dried thyme
- Salt and pepper to taste

**Instructions**:

- Preheat the air fryer to 400°F (204°C).
- Brush the salmon fillets with olive oil and sprinkle with lemon zest, thyme, salt, and pepper.
- Place the fillets in the air fryer basket, skin side down.
- Cook for 8–10 minutes, depending on thickness, until the salmon is flaky and fully cooked.
- Serve with lemon wedges and your favorite side dishes.

**Nutritional Information (per serving)**:

- Calories: 350
- Fat: 20g
- Carbs: 0g

- Protein: 40g

**Cooking Tip**: For extra flavor, marinate the salmon in olive oil, lemon juice, and herbs for 15–30 minutes before cooking.

## Veggie Stir-Fry

**Ingredients:**

- 1 red bell pepper, sliced
- 1 zucchini, sliced
- ½ cup broccoli florets
- 1 tablespoon of soy sauce
- 1 tablespoon of sesame oil
- ½ teaspoon of garlic powder
- ½ teaspoon of ginger powder

**Instructions:**

- Preheat the air fryer to 375°F (190°C).
- Toss the vegetables with soy sauce, sesame oil, garlic powder, and ginger powder.
- Place the vegetables in the air fryer basket and cook for 8–10 minutes, shaking halfway through.
- Serve over rice or noodles for a quick meal.

**Nutritional Information (per serving):**

- Calories: 120
- Fat: 7g
- Carbs: 15g
- Protein: 3g

**Cooking Tip**: Add tofu or shrimp to the stir-fry for extra protein.

## Stuffed Bell Peppers

**Ingredients:**

- 4 bell peppers, tops cut off and seeds removed
- 1 cup of cooked quinoa or rice
- ½ pound of ground turkey or beef
- ¼ cup shredded cheese (optional)
- 1 teaspoon chili powder
- Salt and pepper to taste

**Instructions:**

- Preheat the air fryer to 370°F (188°C).
- In a pan, brown the ground turkey or beef with chili powder, salt, and pepper.
- Mix the cooked quinoa or rice with the browned meat and stuff the bell peppers with the mixture.
- Sprinkle cheese on top if desired.
- Place the stuffed peppers in the air fryer basket and cook for 15–18 minutes until the peppers are tender.

**Nutritional Information (per serving):**

- Calories: 300
- Fat: 14g

- Carbs: 20g
- Protein: 22g

**Cooking Tip**: If you want a softer pepper, you can pre-cook the peppers for 5 minutes before stuffing them.

Mastering Air Fryer Magic

## Chicken Fajitas

**Ingredients:**

- 2 chicken breasts, thinly sliced
- 1 red onion, sliced
- 1 red bell pepper, sliced
- 1 tablespoon of olive oil
- 1 tablespoon of fajita seasoning
- Flour tortillas (for serving)

**Instructions:**

- Preheat the air fryer to 375°F (190°C).
- Toss the chicken, onion, and bell pepper with olive oil and fajita seasoning.
- Place the chicken and veggies in the air fryer basket and cook for 15–18 minutes, shaking halfway through.
- Serve in warm tortillas with your favorite toppings.

**Nutritional Information (per serving):**

- Calories: 250
- Fat: 12g
- Carbs: 18g
- Protein: 22g

**Cooking Tip**: For a smoky flavor, use chipotle fajita seasoning.

## Meatballs

**Ingredients:**

- ½ pound of ground beef or turkey
- ¼ cup of breadcrumbs
- 1 egg
- 1 teaspoon of garlic powder
- 1 teaspoon of dried oregano
- Salt and pepper to taste

**Instructions:**

- Preheat the air fryer to 375°F (190°C).
- In a bowl, mix all ingredients together and form into 1-inch meatballs.
- Place the meatballs in the air fryer basket in a single layer.
- Cook for 10–12 minutes, turning halfway through, until the meatballs are cooked through and golden brown.
- Serve with pasta or as an appetizer with marinara sauce.

**Nutritional Information (per serving):**

- Calories: 200
- Fat: 12g
- Carbs: 8g

- Protein: 18g

**Cooking Tip**: Add some grated Parmesan cheese to the meatball mixture for extra flavor.

## BBQ Chicken Breasts

**Ingredients:**

- 2 chicken breasts
- ¼ cup of barbecue sauce
- 1 tablespoon of olive oil
- Salt and pepper to taste

**Instructions:**

- Preheat the air fryer to 375°F (190°C).
- Rub the chicken breasts with olive oil, salt, and pepper.
- Brush barbecue sauce on both sides of the chicken.
- Cook for 20–25 minutes, flipping halfway through, until the internal temperature reaches 165°F (74°C).
- Serve with extra barbecue sauce and your favorite sides.

**Nutritional Information (per serving):**

- Calories: 280
- Fat: 10g
- Carbs: 8g
- Protein: 36g

**Cooking Tip**: For a caramelized sauce, brush on more barbecue sauce during the last few minutes of cooking.

# CHAPTER 7: AIR FRYER FOR SPECIAL DIETS

## Introduction to Special Diets and Air Fryer Cooking

Air fryers are versatile and can be adapted for various dietary needs, including keto, vegan, gluten-free, and low-carb diets. In this chapter, we'll explore how you can use the air fryer to create dishes that meet specific dietary preferences and restrictions without compromising on taste or texture.

## Keto Chicken Wings

**Ingredients**:

- 8 chicken wings
- 1 tablespoon of olive oil
- 1 teaspoon of garlic powder
- 1 teaspoon of paprika
- Salt and pepper to taste

**Instructions**:

- Preheat the air fryer to 380°F (193°C).
- Rub the chicken wings with olive oil, garlic powder, paprika, salt, and pepper.
- Arrange the wings in the air fryer basket and cook for 20–25 minutes, shaking halfway through.
- Serve with a side of low-carb dipping sauce.

**Nutritional Information (per serving)**:

- Calories: 220
- Fat: 14g
- Carbs: 1g
- Protein: 24g

**Cooking Tip**: For extra crispiness, cook the wings skin-side down for the first half of cooking.

## Vegan Tofu Bites

**Ingredients:**

- 1 block firm tofu, pressed and cut into cubes
- 1 tablespoon of soy sauce
- 1 teaspoon of garlic powder
- ½ teaspoon of smoked paprika
- 1 tablespoon of cornstarch

**Instructions:**

- Preheat the air fryer to 375°F (190°C).
- Toss the tofu cubes in soy sauce, garlic powder, paprika, and cornstarch.
- Place the tofu in the air fryer basket and cook for 15–20 minutes, shaking halfway through.
- Serve with a dipping sauce or add to a salad.

**Nutritional Information (per serving):**

- Calories: 180
- Fat: 10g
- Carbs: 8g
- Protein: 16g

**Cooking Tip:** Use a non-stick spray to avoid sticking and ensure crispy edges.

Mastering Air Fryer Magic

## Gluten-Free French Fries

**Ingredients:**

- 4 medium potatoes, cut into fries
- 2 tablespoons of olive oil
- ½ teaspoon of garlic powder
- Salt to taste

**Instructions:**

- Preheat the air fryer to 380°F (193°C).
- Toss the potato fries with olive oil, garlic powder, and salt.
- Place the fries in a single layer in the air fryer basket and cook for 15–18 minutes, shaking halfway through.
- Serve with your favorite gluten-free dipping sauce.

**Nutritional Information (per serving):**

- Calories: 150
- Fat: 7g
- Carbs: 22g
- Protein: 3g

**Cooking Tip:** Soak the potato fries in water for 30 minutes before cooking for a crispier result.

## Low-Carb Zucchini Chips

**Ingredients**:

- 2 zucchinis, sliced thinly
- 1 tablespoon of olive oil
- ¼ teaspoon of garlic powder
- Salt and pepper to taste

**Instructions**:

- Preheat the air fryer to 375°F (190°C).
- Toss the zucchini slices in olive oil, garlic powder, salt, and pepper.
- Arrange the slices in a single layer in the air fryer basket and cook for 8–10 minutes, until crispy.
- Serve with a low-carb dip or enjoy on their own.

**Nutritional Information (per serving)**:

- Calories: 70
- Fat: 4g
- Carbs: 8g
- Protein: 2g

**Cooking Tip**: For extra crispiness, don't overcrowd the basket, and cook in batches if necessary.

## Paleo Sweet Potato Fries

**Ingredients:**

- 2 medium sweet potatoes, cut into fries
- 1 tablespoon of coconut oil, melted
- ½ teaspoon of paprika
- Salt to taste

**Instructions:**

- Preheat the air fryer to 380°F (193°C).
- Toss the sweet potato fries in melted coconut oil, paprika, and salt.
- Arrange in a single layer in the air fryer basket.
- Cook for 15–18 minutes, shaking halfway through, until crispy.

**Nutritional Information (per serving):**

- Calories: 160
- Fat: 7g
- Carbs: 22g
- Protein: 2g

**Cooking Tip:** If you like your fries extra crispy, flip them halfway through cooking.

## Dairy-Free Chocolate Cake

**Ingredients:**

- 1 cup all-purpose flour (gluten-free if necessary)
- ½ cup of cocoa powder
- ½ cup of sugar
- 1 teaspoon of baking soda
- ½ teaspoon of salt
- ½ cup of almond milk
- ¼ cup of vegetable oil

**Instructions:**

- Preheat the air fryer to 350°F (175°C).
- Mix all the dry ingredients together, then add the almond milk and vegetable oil.
- Pour the batter into a greased air fryer-safe baking pan.
- Cook for 12–15 minutes, checking with a toothpick to ensure it's done.
- Serve with dairy-free whipped cream or chocolate frosting.

**Nutritional Information (per serving):**

- Calories: 250
- Fat: 14g
- Carbs: 30g
- Protein: 3g

**Cooking Tip**: Let the cake cool completely before frosting to prevent it from melting.

## Low-Carb Chicken Parmesan

**Ingredients:**

- 2 chicken breasts
- ½ cup of almond flour
- 1 egg, beaten
- 1 cup of marinara sauce (sugar-free)
- ¼ cup shredded mozzarella cheese

**Instructions:**

- Preheat the air fryer to 375°F (190°C).
- Dredge the chicken breasts in almond flour, then dip in egg.
- Place the chicken in the air fryer basket and cook for 12–15 minutes.
- Top with marinara sauce and mozzarella cheese, then cook for an additional 2-3 minutes until the cheese melts.
- Serve with a side of zucchini noodles.

**Nutritional Information (per serving):**

- Calories: 300
- Fat: 15g
- Carbs: 8g
- Protein: 40g

Mastering Air Fryer Magic

**Cooking Tip**: You can add Parmesan cheese for an extra cheesy topping.

# CHAPTER 8: AIR FRYER SIDES AND SNACKS

## Introduction to Air Fryer Sides and Snacks

Sides and snacks can elevate any meal, and the air fryer is perfect for creating crispy, flavorful options without a lot of oil. Whether you're looking for something to pair with a main dish or a quick snack between meals, the air fryer offers a variety of possibilities. This chapter will guide you through some of the best side dishes and snacks that you can make with ease.

## Garlic Parmesan Potato Wedges

**Ingredients:**

- 4 medium russet potatoes, cut into wedges
- 2 tablespoons of olive oil
- 2 tablespoons of grated Parmesan cheese
- 1 teaspoon of garlic powder
- 1 teaspoon of dried rosemary
- Salt and pepper to taste

Mastering Air Fryer Magic

## Instructions:

- Preheat the air fryer to 400°F (204°C).
- Toss the potato wedges in olive oil, Parmesan cheese, garlic powder, rosemary, salt, and pepper.
- Arrange the wedges in the air fryer basket, ensuring they're not overcrowded.
- Cook for 18–20 minutes, shaking the basket halfway through.
- Serve hot with your favorite dipping sauce.

## Nutritional Information (per serving):

- Calories: 230
- Fat: 12g
- Carbs: 28g
- Protein: 5g

**Cooking Tip**: For extra crispiness, soak the potato wedges in water for 30 minutes before cooking.

## Crispy Brussels Sprouts

**Ingredients:**

- 1 lb Brussels sprouts, trimmed and halved
- 2 tablespoons of olive oil
- Salt and pepper to taste
- 1 tablespoon of balsamic vinegar (optional)

**Instructions:**

- Preheat the air fryer to 375°F (190°C).
- Toss the Brussels sprouts with olive oil, salt, and pepper.
- Place them in the air fryer basket and cook for 15–18 minutes, shaking halfway through.
- Drizzle with balsamic vinegar before serving for added flavor.

**Nutritional Information (per serving):**

- Calories: 130
- Fat: 9g
- Carbs: 14g
- Protein: 5g

**Cooking Tip**: For a sweeter touch, drizzle a bit of honey on the Brussels sprouts before serving.

## Sweet Potato Fries

**Ingredients:**

- 2 medium sweet potatoes, cut into fries
- 2 tablespoons of olive oil
- 1 teaspoon of smoked paprika
- Salt and pepper to taste

**Instructions:**

- Preheat the air fryer to 380°F (193°C).
- Toss the sweet potato fries with olive oil, paprika, salt, and pepper.
- Arrange the fries in the air fryer basket and cook for 15–18 minutes, shaking halfway through.
- Serve with a dipping sauce or as a side to your main dish.

**Nutritional Information (per serving):**

- Calories: 150
- Fat: 7g
- Carbs: 22g
- Protein: 2g

**Cooking Tip:** To make the fries extra crispy, soak them in water for 30 minutes before cooking.

## Zucchini Fries

**Ingredients:**

- 2 zucchinis, sliced into fries
- ½ cup of breadcrumbs
- ¼ cup of grated Parmesan cheese
- 1 egg, beaten
- Salt and pepper to taste

**Instructions:**

- Preheat the air fryer to 375°F (190°C).
- In a bowl, combine breadcrumbs, Parmesan cheese, salt, and pepper.
- Dip the zucchini slices into the beaten egg, then coat them with the breadcrumb mixture.
- Arrange the zucchini fries in the air fryer basket and cook for 10–12 minutes, flipping halfway through.
- Serve with marinara sauce for dipping.

**Nutritional Information (per serving):**

- Calories: 140
- Fat: 8g
- Carbs: 14g

- Protein: 5g

**Cooking Tip**: You can season the breadcrumb mixture with herbs like basil or oregano for extra flavor.

## Baked Potatoes

**Ingredients:**

- 4 medium russet potatoes
- 2 tablespoons of olive oil
- Salt and pepper to taste

**Instructions:**

- Preheat the air fryer to 400°F (204°C).
- Rub the potatoes with olive oil, salt, and pepper.
- Place the potatoes in the air fryer basket and cook for 30–35 minutes, turning halfway through.
- Slice open and serve with your favorite toppings.

**Nutritional Information (per serving):**

- Calories: 150
- Fat: 7g
- Carbs: 26g
- Protein: 3g

**Cooking Tip:** For a crispy skin, use a fork to poke holes in the potatoes before air frying.

## Popcorn

**Ingredients:**

- ¼ cup of popcorn kernels
- 1 tablespoon of olive oil
- Salt to taste

**Instructions:**

- Preheat the air fryer to 400°F (204°C).
- Toss the popcorn kernels with olive oil and place them in the air fryer basket.
- Cook for 8–10 minutes, shaking the basket halfway through to ensure even popping.
- Season with salt before serving.

**Nutritional Information (per serving):**

- Calories: 120
- Fat: 5g
- Carbs: 15g
- Protein: 3g

**Cooking Tip**: Use a heat-safe dish or foil in the air fryer basket if you're concerned about kernels escaping.

# CHAPTER 9: AIR FRYER DESSERTS

## Introduction to Air Fryer Desserts

The air fryer isn't just for savory dishes, it can be used to create amazing desserts that are quick, easy, and perfectly portioned. From gooey cakes to crispy cookies, you'll find that the air fryer is your secret weapon for making desserts with less oil and less hassle. In this chapter, we'll explore some delicious dessert recipes you can make in the air fryer.

## Chocolate Lava Cakes

**Ingredients:**

- ½ cup of dark chocolate chips
- ¼ cup of butter
- 2 tablespoons of sugar
- ¼ teaspoon of vanilla extract
- 2 large eggs
- ¼ cup of flour

**Instructions:**

- Preheat the air fryer to 375°F (190°C).
- Melt the chocolate chips and butter together in the microwave.
- In a separate bowl, whisk together the eggs, sugar, and vanilla extract.
- Stir the melted chocolate mixture into the egg mixture, then fold in the flour.
- Pour the batter into greased ramekins and cook for 8–10 minutes, or until the sides are set but the center is still soft.
- Let cool for a minute, then carefully invert the cakes onto plates and serve.

**Nutritional Information (per serving):**

- Calories: 250
- Fat: 18g
- Carbs: 25g
- Protein: 4g

**Cooking Tip**: To make the lava cakes even more decadent, serve them with a scoop of vanilla ice cream.

## Apple Fritters

**Ingredients:**

- 2 medium apples, peeled and diced
- 1 cup all-purpose flour
- ¼ cup of sugar
- 1 teaspoon of cinnamon
- ½ teaspoon of baking powder
- ¼ cup of milk
- 1 egg
- 2 tablespoons of butter, melted

**Instructions:**

- Preheat the air fryer to 350°F (175°C).
- In a bowl, combine the flour, sugar, cinnamon, and baking powder.
- Add the milk, egg, and melted butter, then stir in the diced apples.
- Drop spoonfuls of the batter into the air fryer basket, making sure they're not touching.
- Cook for 8–10 minutes, flipping halfway through, until golden brown.
- Dust with powdered sugar before serving.

**Nutritional Information (per serving):**

- Calories: 190

Mastering Air Fryer Magic

- Fat: 9g
- Carbs: 26g
- Protein: 2g

**Cooking Tip**: For extra flavor, drizzle with caramel sauce or sprinkle with cinnamon sugar after cooking.

Mastering Air Fryer Magic

## Banana Bread

**Ingredients:**

- 2 ripe bananas, mashed
- 1 cup of flour
- ¼ cup of sugar
- ¼ cup of butter, melted
- 1 egg
- ½ teaspoon of baking powder
- ¼ teaspoon of cinnamon

**Instructions:**

- Preheat the air fryer to 320°F (160°C).
- In a bowl, mix the mashed bananas, flour, sugar, butter, egg, baking powder, and cinnamon until smooth.
- Pour the batter into a greased baking pan that fits in the air fryer basket.
- Cook for 25–30 minutes, or until a toothpick comes out clean.
- Let cool before slicing.

**Nutritional Information (per serving):**

- Calories: 180
- Fat: 8g
- Carbs: 25g

- Protein: 3g

**Cooking Tip**: Add chocolate chips or walnuts to the batter for a different twist.

# CONCLUSION

## Mastering the Magic of Air Frying

Congratulations on reaching the end of this journey into the world of air frying! By now, you've learned how to master the air fryer, create delicious and crispy meals, and discover how this versatile kitchen appliance can help you cook healthier and tastier dishes with ease. Whether you're cooking quick snacks, savory mains, or indulgent desserts, the air fryer is a fantastic tool that makes meal preparation simpler and faster without sacrificing flavor or texture.

As you continue to explore air frying, remember that the key to success is experimenting with ingredients, techniques, and flavors to find your personal favorites. The air fryer's magic lies in its ability to cook food quickly while preserving its natural taste and texture, offering endless possibilities for creativity in the kitchen.

## Tips for Continuing Your Air Fryer Journey

Mastering Air Fryer Magic

- **Experiment**: Don't hesitate to try new recipes and ingredients. The air fryer is versatile, and once you get comfortable, you can adapt many traditional recipes to work in the air fryer.
- **Use Fresh Ingredients**: For the best results, use fresh and high-quality ingredients. This will ensure that your meals are not only healthier but also packed with flavor.
- **Clean Your Air Fryer Regularly**: A clean air fryer ensures that your meals come out perfect every time. Make sure to clean the basket and tray after each use to maintain optimal performance.
- **Adjust Cooking Times**: Every air fryer model is slightly different, so don't be afraid to adjust cooking times and temperatures as needed based on your specific appliance.
- **Don't Overcrowd**: For the crispiest results, avoid overcrowding the basket. Giving your food enough space allows the hot air to circulate evenly, ensuring the perfect crisp every time.

Air frying is more than just a cooking method; it's an opportunity to embrace a healthier, faster, and more enjoyable way of preparing meals. By following the techniques and recipes outlined in this book, you are now equipped to create delicious dishes for every occasion, from simple weekday meals to impressive dinners and desserts.

We hope that this cookbook has inspired you to embrace the full potential of the air fryer and transform your kitchen into a place of creativity and culinary delight. The recipes shared here are just the beginning—continue to explore, experiment, and, most importantly, enjoy every moment of cooking!

## Thank You for Choosing Air Fryer Magic!

Remember, the real magic of cooking comes from the joy of creating meals that bring people together. Whether you're cooking for family, friends, or just yourself, the air fryer is your partner in delivering crispy, crunchy, and irresistible dishes every time.

Happy air frying!

Made in United States
North Haven, CT
31 March 2025